EMOTIONAL INTELLIGENCE SPECTRUM
Explore Your Emotions and Improve Your Intrapersonal Intelligence

BY JOSHUA MOORE

The Emotional Intelligence Spectrum

Find out where you currently fall on the spectrum of Emotional Intelligence and what this signifies.

Learn how to navigate the spectrum and reposition yourself at a higher point, through mind-body reconnection, in order to achieve higher emotional intelligence and success in business and personal relationships.

FREE DOWNLOAD

INSIGHTFUL GROWTH STRATEGIES FOR YOUR PERSONAL AND PROFESSIONAL SUCCESS!

amazonkindle   nook   kobo   iBooks
Windows   android   BlackBerry

Sign up here to get a free copy of Growth Games workbook and more:

www.frenchnumber.net/growth

TABLE OF CONTENTS

Introduction 6

Identifying who and where you are on the Emotional Intelligence Spectrum 11
- EMOTIONAL INTELLIGENCE TEST 11
- Your EI Test Results, and What They Mean 27
- How Emotional Intelligence Identities are "judged" in our society 33
- The reasons we are positioned where we are on the EI Spectrum 37
- How Did I End Up Here? 37
- Reconnect, Reset, Reposition! 47
- DENIAL, DISTRACTION AND DRUDGERY 53

A Practical Implementation Guide 55
- Business EI 57
- EI and Leadership 58
- EI and Workflow 61
- EI and Networking 63
- EI and Conflict Resolution 65
- EI and Career Path 67
- Work/Personal Relationships and EI 69
- Using EI to Influence Others 70
- Using EI to be a Better Communicator 73
- Work Relationships and EI 74
- Friendships and EI 77
- Romantic Relationships and EI 79
- Family Relationships and EI 81

Self-Improvement EI 83

Using EI to be More Social 84
Using EI to be More Successful 85
Using EI to Gain Self-Control...86
Using EI to be Fulfilled 87

Review and Summary.. 89
Interrelating your worlds into a cohesive whole 89

Bonus Chapter 30 Day EI Immersion Program.......... 92

Introduction

Emotional Intelligence, EI, Emotional Quotient, EQ, Intrapersonal Relations... All these phrases and more are used in the workplace, seminars, workshops, therapy sessions as well as mindfulness trainings and meditation videos every day around the globe. What they all mean is the variable ability to identify, understand and control the feelings of self and others, in order to succeed in all walks of life.

Considering the amount that has been written about Emotional Intelligence in recent years, I think it is of the utmost importance to clarify what is different about this book, and more importantly, what this book will impart, that will give you the ability to improve the quality of your work and personal lives. I believe what sets this book apart is the notion that Emotional Intelligence falls on a spectrum, with four major points and many variations and combinations of those points along its path. I have identified these four major points as follows: EU, or Emotionally Unavailable; EE, or Emotional Empath; EE, or Emotionally Enlightened and II, Id Intelligence.

Let's define these four points of Emotional Intelligence. EU, or Emotionally Unavailable, is pretty self-explanatory. Through any number of reasons, which we will explore later in section one of this book, an individual who has no idea how he feels or how anyone around him feels is Emotionally Unavailable. This would be considered the low point on the EI spectrum, or to be more optimistic, the starting point. EE, or Emotional Enlightenment, conversely, would be the mecca, or high point of the EI spectrum. It represents an ideal state of Emotional Intelligence, where the emotions of self and others are completely available, controllable, transparent, and able to interconnect with one another through an effortless flow. EE, or an Emotional Empath, is anyone who is able to discern the feelings of others to a point where it almost appears they are obsessed and hypervigilant about them. Ironically, this leaves them emotionally depleted and unable and/or unwilling to identify what they are feeling, except for seemingly unsourced anxiety, resentment and rage. Finally, II; one who is Id Intelligent, or as I like to think of it , "Id's all about me!", is represented by the individual who is absolutely in tune with her feelings to the exclusion of all others. Yet, despite this self-centered approach, the II person still feels empty, hurt and frustrated.

I also believe that the EI spectrum follows a circular path, and that three of the four major points, if seen on a three set Venn diagram would look like this:

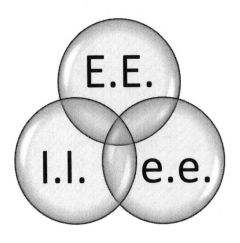

Notice how these three very different states of emotional intelligence overlap and how close they are despite their differences. Emotional Enlightenment (EE), or the ideal we all, as human beings should be striving toward, is actually the product of a precise balance between being an Emotional Empath (ee) and being id intelligent (II), neither of which are desirable emotional intelligence states on their own. So close and yet so far!

I envision this cluster of 3 at the top of a circular path, starting from either side, either with II or ee, and following, quickly in both cases with EU. Both of these paths travel separately to the bottom of the circle, where they meet, join as one and begin to climb and grow like a tree, up through the center of the circle towards EE, as is represented by the following graphic:

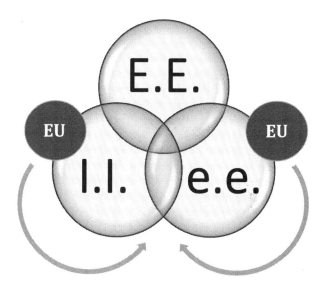

The intent of this book will be to define where you are on the EI spectrum, figure out how you got there, explore the possibility of a mind/body disconnect and how to repair it, learn about situational and relational EI, discuss 3 major factors and impediments to EI growth, and finally how to implement all of this knowledge and reposition yourself high up on the EI spectrum to ensure success in your work and personal life! I am excited to share this information with you because I've been on my own EI journey and I know it works!

Part One

Identifying who and where you are on the Emotional Intelligence Spectrum

In order to allow you to figure out who and where you are on the EI spectrum, I have devised a simple 24 question test. If you are as honest as you can be, when taking it, this should give you a solid starting point on your EI journey without having to ask others for personal feedback.

EMOTIONAL INTELLIGENCE TEST

Circle the answer nearest to how you feel.

Q1. When I enter a meeting at work I feel:

- A. Ready to go to battle. I have my agenda and my goal is to get my needs met.
- B. Worried about different people and the conflict that is bound to rise between them. I hope I can help them fix their differences
- C. I try to go without expectations. I am prepared and know what will be

discussed and my goals are to gain better understanding and help come up with solutions that will benefit all of us.

D. Detached. Meetings are pointless and I have a hard time concentrating.

Q2. It's time for my annual review. I feel:

A. On the defense. I've done a great job this year, no thanks to anyone else, and I'd better be getting what I deserve.

B. Anxious. I've spent the last year doing everything everyone told me and being "the diplomat". This is the third year I haven't gotten a raise or a promotion. It just doesn't make sense!

C. Ready to listen and respond positively, politely and honestly. I have a pretty good idea of what my strengths and weaknesses are, but I am interested to hear someone else's view.

D. Defeated. I really don't care. I'll be "happy" If I'm not fired or put on another probation.

Q3. There's a job opening at a higher level in my department:

A. No question this should be my job. They owe me and I'm going to make sure everyone knows it.
B. I went to my boss and asked what she thought about my chances. She said it wasn't that I wasn't qualified, but I'm so good at what I do now, she couldn't possibly move me at this point. I had to leave her office because I couldn't keep from crying.
C. I've made an appointment with my boss, who I've already told I'm interested in applying for the new job. I will go to the meeting with talking points about why getting this job will be good for the department and for myself.
D. Why bother?

Q4. My Team at work is 4 days late with a project and we've just been called on the carpet by the manager:

A. I blow up. I'm not taking this abuse. I had great ideas but no one cared. I'm not going down with this ship. I'm naming names and covering my butt.
B. I try to explain how everyone feels about us being late, and the rest of the team turns against me. How could they do this

to me when I was just trying to protect them?
C. I listen to what the manager is saying, and start taking notes, suggesting that we all work out a revised schedule in order to complete the project as soon as possible.
D. I think about what I'm going to watch on Netflix tonight. The boss asks me a question, and I have to ask him to repeat it…

Q5. We're having a team building day at work:

A. Personally, I don't need this time wasting crap, but since I'm here, I have lots to say about stuff that needs to change!
B. I try and listen to what everyone wants, and I'm always there to interpret people's feelings to the trainer when I don't think he's getting what others are really trying to say. At the end of the day, I'm exhausted and hurt because I heard a couple of people making fun of me at the break.
C. I make notes on the outline, actively listen and participate in whatever is on the agenda. I've made it my goal to be

in the moment today and get as much out of the training as I can.

D. I fell asleep 3 times after lunch. I cannot keep my eyes open!

Q6. The new boss is having individual meetings this week:

A. Finally! I'm going in there and telling her exactly what's been going on around here. She needs to know how valuable I am and how everyone else has been screwing off.

B. I want her to know that I am here for her and anything she needs help with, I can do it. I really understand the dynamic of this place and get all the different personalities. People can be mean or spiteful, but they really don't mean it. Can't we all just get along? She asks me what I'd like in the way of personal job growth, and I go blank. My throat closes up and I feel dizzy.

C. I listen to her questions, trying to answer them as honestly but professionally as possible. I do everything in my power not to talk about other people, as I believe this meeting truly is an opportunity to get to know one another better.

D. I totally forget we are supposed to meet and show up 10 minutes late. She's on a call and says we will have to reschedule. Whatever…

Q.7 When it's time to get together with friends, I like to:

A. Either get together with a gang of people and be the center of attention, or hang out with one person and tell them everything that's been going on in my life. My friends need to interest me. I don't have time to be bored and hear them moan and groan.
B. I'm that friend that is a great listener, and I'm always willing to lend a hand and help you out. Sometimes I wish I had a friend like me, lol. Also, I'm not great at being with two friends at once. I get too worried they might not get along.
C. I try and keep up with a wide circle of friends and acquaintances. Obviously there are friends who are closer than others, but I enjoy socializing with a variety of people and learning about their lives.
D. Most times I keep to myself. It just doesn't seem worth the bother.

Q8. The quality I most value in friendship is:

A. Someone who "gets" me. What you see is what you get. Take me as I am.
B. Someone who needs me. I want to feel like an important part of your life. I'm always looking for people to be part of my "family".
C. Someone I can give and take with. We don't have to think the same about everything; that makes life more interesting. It's more important that I can trust you and that you feel the same way.
D. Low maintenance. I don't want to feel obligated or depended upon.

Q9. My two best friends are fighting:

A. I'm annoyed. I need them to get along. I don't have time for this.
B. I'm devastated. I can't sleep. I don't know whose side to be on. Why can't I fix them?
C. I give them both space, to come to me when and as they want. I try to see both sides of the issue, but at the end of the day, I need to respect that this is a problem between the 2 of them.
D. They probably wouldn't tell me. I'm not much good at "feeling" stuff.

Q10. My best friend's wife has asked me to plan a 40th birthday party:

    A. To tell you the truth, I didn't know we were "best friends"! What a drag! Oh well, I guess I'll just put together all the stuff I like to do. At least I'll have a good time.

    B. I am obviously honored, but also completely overwhelmed. I want this to be perfect but how can I make sure this happens? Some of the people I've invited aren't coming and I am freaking out.

    C. I put together a crack "birthday" team of some of our friends, work out who's responsible for what and have as much fun planning the event as the event itself.

    D. I look out the window and pretend I didn't hear her.

Q11. I tend to have lifelong friendships because:

    A. Actually, it's really not up to me how long you're my friend. Don't cross me or piss me off and we'll be lifelong friends. Otherwise, it's time to move on.

B. I really value lifelong friendships, but as I get older, I've had some people who I thought I was close to, abandon me. Some of them even seem to resent me for some reason. I give everything to my friends, but I guess maybe you never really know how some people are.
C. I've learned to choose friends who will grow with me through the years. We trust each other with our feelings and also respect healthy boundaries.
D. As long as someone wants to be friends with me and doesn't need all sorts of "maintenance", it is what it is.

Q12. When I fight with a friend:

A. It's not pretty and it's not going to end well if they don't admit they're wrong. I only fight with friends when they mess with me, and I don't give second chances very often.
B. It feels like I'm breaking apart. It consumes every moment of my day, until either they forgive me or they stop communicating with me. I can't let it alone and take it as a personal failure.
C. I give myself time and space not only to see where I am coming from but to see where my friend is coming from.

Hopefully we can always come to an understanding, but I know that in the end, I can only fix my side of it and respectfully hold space for my friend.

D. Frankly, it would be highly unlikely. I don't have the energy to fight. I suppose you could get mad AT me, but you wouldn't get much of response. Sorry. Not sorry.

Q13. If I described my family dynamic:

A. I'm definitely the leader of the pack. My family may not always like me but they love me or at least respect me.

B. I have issues with my family. It seems all I do is give and all they do is take. All I've ever wanted is a loving, happy family but I always seem to end up the odd man out.

C. My family dynamic is fluid, because it is made up of individuals with commonalities and differences. What holds it together is love, respect and understanding, which takes constant maintenance to run relatively smoothly.

D. My family puts up with me. They are used to me. I don't change, for better or worse.

Q14. If my family described me they'd say:

A. I've been through a lot and I've learned not to let anyone get in my way. You may not always like me, but you'll always know how I feel.
B. Sometimes I'm afraid my family thinks I'm a pushover or a doormat. I'm always an afterthought, unless they need something. Then they know I'll always be there for them.
C. I think they'd all have good and bad things to say, if I were to be honest. I know how I feel about all of them, as individuals and as a family unit. We are a work in progress and so am I.
D. Good ole' so and so. S/he might not be much, but s/he's ours.

Q15. My Perfect Love Match would be:

A. Someone who always had my back; who believes in me and doesn't want to "change" or "fix" me.
B. Someone who could wave a magic wand and make me feel calm and happy! Someone who really wants to know me!
C. Someone I could take the rest of my life to get to know more and more

intimately. Someone I could grow with and share my life experiences with.
D. I have no idea...

Q16. My technique for dealing with family conflict could be described as:

    A. My way or the highway. I fight to win. I don't lose. Ever.
    B. I tend to start out trying to understand everyone's side, but often I become overwhelmed and flooded with emotion. Sometimes when I cry, everyone assumes I'm sad...but secretly I'm really angry.
    C. I always try to remember that these people are, and need to always remain, members of my family. With this in mind, I try and listen with respect, add my own views when appropriate and help figure out the best resolution for all involved.
    D. Duck and cover. Conflict wipes me out.

Q17. True or False? When I am wrong, I apologize:

    A. False. I don't apologize. It's a sign of weakness. Just move on!
    B. True! I always apologize, sometimes even when it's not my fault. It's almost a

knee jerk reaction. I just want everyone to be happy!

C. When I apologize, I make every effort to be sincere and to own what it is I am apologizing for. I don't twist the apology, or have the last word or act like I'm being forced to do it.

D. If it'll make you leave me alone, ok, I'm sorry.

Q18. When Disciplining Children:

A. Normally, I don't deal with that stuff. If forced, I keep it short and not so sweet. I find if you tell them like it is, they don't tend to come back for a second helping. You're never too young to learn how unfair life can be. I'm no monster, but I don't mince words.

B. It breaks my heart when my kids do something wrong. How could they do that to me? I'm so nice to them! I've noticed, as they've gotten older they don't seem to care as much when I cry or get sad that they've misbehaved.

C. I don't do or say anything until I've had few moments to calm down. I'm the adult. I have to act like an adult. I think about where they are at in their short lives and try to really understand WHY

they did what they did. There are no set rules or one punishment fits all.
D. I can't even deal with this stuff. Not my strong suit.

Q19. When I envision my perfect life I see:

A. Everything going my way at last! Finally getting the respect and notice and rewards I deserve!
B. Peace. Nobody fighting. Calmness. People understanding what I want. ME understanding what I want…
C. It's not so much something I'll just see. I'll feel it too. Life will flow; everyone and everything will work together.
D. Me understanding what I want… and deserve! I try to really understand WHY possibility of life actually improving hasn't occurred to me in a very long time.

Q20. I wake up in the morning:

A. On the warpath. I've already mentally gone down my current list of enemies and I face the day, armed for the conflicts sure to arise.
B. With a knot in my stomach. I wake up sometimes not even able to identify

what I'm anxious about. It is a chronic state of mind.
C. Rested and ready to give myself a few minutes to awaken as I look forward to all the things I like to do and acknowledge the things I need to do in the day that lies open before me.
D. Really tired.

Q21. The thing I look forward to most every day is:

A. When I get positive feedback from something I've done. I look forward to it, but it doesn't happen very often!
B. Getting home after a long day and escaping to a hot bath.
C. Accomplishing goals; interacting with people in a positive way; learning something new; spending time with friends and family
D. Going back to bed.

Q22. If I had one wish to be granted:

A. To finally be acknowledged as the best.
B. To finally be acknowledged as the kindest.

C. To be given 100 more years of this life, and the health to enjoy it!

D. I need more time to think about this

Q23. If I could change one thing in my life:

A. I would stop having to fight for everything I care for in life.

B. I would stop caring so much about everyone else and what they thought of me.

C. I would be financially independent enough to spend more of my time learning and understanding others and enjoying my family and friends.

D. I would actually know what I'd like to change!

Q24. Sometimes, when I go to sleep at night:

A. I go over every conflict I had during the day: every slight, every insult; and I plan my sweet revenge.

B. I lay awake for hours going over every embarrassing mistake I've ever made, all the way back to my childhood

C. I am grateful for another day, good and bad, and fall asleep knowing I've done the best I could.

D. I don't even get through one episode of "Friends" before I fall into a coma.

Now simply add up how many of each letter (A-D) that you got and take your results to the next chapter to figure out where you currently reside on the EI Spectrum.

Your EI Test Results, and What They Mean

As I mentioned earlier, this test was simple in design. If you got more of one letter than the others, then you lean more heavily towards one of the four Emotional Intelligence points I described in the introduction of this book. If you scored more evenly between 2 or more letters, it just means you are either between two of the major points, and /or presented with different emotional intelligences at different times, due to situational or relationship factors.

Please understand that I purposely made the answers very broad in character, so that there would be no questions or subtlety when deciding how to answer. Obviously, you, as individual human beings are not replicas of these stock character descriptions.

Also: If you are lucky enough to have scored as Emotionally Enlightened, good for you! I urge you however, to continue reading this book for two reasons.

1. Emotional Enlightenment is a state of balance. Maintenance of this balance is crucial. 2. Enlightenment is never a resting state. It is the ultimate work in progress. Hopefully there will be plenty of material in these pages to further your enlightenment journey!

The Letter Identities are as follows:

A= II, or Id Intelligence

B= ee, or Emotional Empath (lower case "ee" to differentiate from Emotional Enlightenment, EE, as well as to illustrate the loss of self that results from being an Empath.

C= EE, or Emotional Enlightenment

D = EU, or Emotionally Unavailable

So let's now explore each of these categories in further depth. In keeping with my original graphic of the Emotional Intelligence Spectrum using a tree image to represent the major points and pathways to potential growth, I will be describing different trees to visually illustrate some of the more visceral characteristics of these EI identities.

Id Intelligence (II):

Like the large, dominant pine tree I have chosen to represent this EI identity, people who exhibit Id Intelligence are hyper aware of their own needs and feelings, to the extent that they literally crowd out and overshadow other people around them. Because they can be aggressive in meeting their needs, they appear to be strong and hearty souls who flourish despite little input from others. If we look more closely, however, much of this strength and intimidation is often defensive posturing, brought on to head off any potential attack at the very outset. If you stand under a large enough pine tree, you'll notice the ground beneath it is barren, as its heavy and spiky branches, needles and cones preclude any sunlight, rain or nutrients from penetrating its heavy mantle. In the same way, Id Intelligent types can take the air out of a room, leaving nothing for mere mortals to breathe in or out. Because of this, they are often thought of as bullies, ring leaders, or trouble makers, and their behavioral "prickliness" often keeps others at a distance. Still standing beneath the mighty pine, and this time looking up, you'll notice that many of the inner branches are brittle, brown and dead, suffocated by its own evergreen bulk. The Id intelligent person may seem a solid and foreboding presence, but inside, they may be emotionally disintegrating, from lack of positive relationships and intimacy.

Emotional Empath (ee):

Picture a tree, branches intertwined with the grasping tendrils of an invasive species, leaves, feasted on by parasites, stunted by the elements and other, bigger trees. This tree embodies to me, what it must feel like to be an emotional empath; someone who feels so much for others, that their very essence gradually evaporates, because they have used all of their energy and emotion to feel someone else's emotion. Like the branches, tightly bound by other plants' vines, empaths, named for empathy, or the state of being able to understand and experience the feeling of another, become so involved in other people's emotions, that they are spiritually paralyzed to their own needs and feelings. Empaths typically have poor boundaries, and allow other people to parasitically suck them dry. So busy trying to fix everybody else's problems, the empath doesn't recognize their own depletions until in a stage of chronic yet nameless anxiety. Empaths are so skilled at taking on the emotions of others that they often seem to physically diminish, ignored or forgotten by the very people they "feel" so deeply for, until another crisis occurs and their services are demanded again. Empaths seem to buy into the belief that if they do for everybody what they secretly (even to themselves) crave just ONE person would reciprocate and do for them, the laws of justice will ensure that eventually fair play will occur and their needs will be met. Unfortunately, this reality often is only revealed in the dusty pages of fairy tales.

Emotional Enlightenment (EE):

I can't think of a better representation of Emotional Enlightenment than the graceful, flexible Willow. Besides being aesthetically pleasing to all the senses, it is truly a case of balance in action. Its flowing branches grow from a very shallow root system that is dependent on the firmness of the earth beneath it and precise water ratios for its very survival. Soil erosion or one bad rain storm can topple the biggest or eldest Willow in a matter of minutes. Like the Willow, Emotional Enlightenment is also a tricky balancing act between feelings for self and feelings for others. Maintenance of EE is dependent on the ability to be able to be flexible and adjust your emotional calibration to match the situation or relationship you find yourself in moment by moment. One episode where you are emotionally overwhelmed by your needs or the needs of others can topple you from a state of enlightenment to one of Id or Empath in a matter of minutes.

The elegant willow has a striking presence in any environment, but no matter how large an area its branches cover, there is always ample room for the other elements to flow through and around its verdant, delicate growth. Emotional Enlightenment also allows us to be present without dominating our surroundings or our fellow beings. Enlightenment is never a state of inertia; its very essence depends on continued growth, leaving room for the light of other's to further nourish it. A weeping willow, animated by a spring breeze, reaches out in all directions, never to dominate but to dance with nature. Emotional Enlightenment, activated by presence and a motivation to understand, enables us to reach out, helping ourselves and others in a similar dance of flowing resilience.

Emotionally Unavailable (EU):

A dead tree represents how someone who is Emotionally Unavailable attempts to cut themselves off from self and others, in order to deaden feelings they are unable to process. Ironically, if we were able to cut away this layer of unavailability from EU people, much like the dead branches from a toughened, battered tree, we would most likely uncover deep, visceral emotions with the intensity and power of the mightiest oak. A tree that has been battered by the elements and left to fend for itself, without nourishment and/or protection from the elements, dries up, hardens and dies. A person who has consciously or unconsciously chosen to become Emotionally Unavailable, because of situational, relational or transitional trauma, defensively removes themselves from emotion of any kind, be it from themselves or others. For the Emotionally Unavailable, inertia cloaks them in a protective, if numbing cocoon. The good news is, unlike the tree, which eventually will rot and fall in pieces into the ground from which it came, the Emotionally Unavailable person can, like a phoenix, rise from the ashes of their inertia and experience emotional growth towards enlightenment, through vigilant and consistent accessing of presence and resilience.

How Emotional Intelligence Identities are "judged" in our society

Whether we like it or not, we are living in the age of social media, rife with in-your-face, in-the-moment communication, be it true or "fake" news (but always opinionated), and able to find a common audience, no matter how extreme or outrageous the content. Everyone is a reporter and everyone is a consumer. The lid is off the box and Pandora has run away in helpless horror. An interesting byproduct of social media and its ability to rally any troop, is the juried labeling of every element of the human psyche. I find it fascinating, then, when looking at Emotional Intelligence and its identities to see how they are judged through the lens of social media. It's pretty obvious that anyone who embodies characteristics of Id Intelligence is viewed on Facebook as the bad guy. A hint of being self-serving, and you will be permanently slapped with the Narcissist label; although astoundingly, these very same "bad guys" are currently being lauded by millions as the best men for the job because "they tell it like it is". At a more everyman level, Id Intelligence is defended daily by thousands of posts and memes with the message of "I've been through hell and back and you better not cross me because I'll destroy you'.

On the other hand, the Empath is often celebrated as a sainted victim (often of the Id Intelligent!). These selfless souls are depicted as endlessly used and abused through no fault of their own as they march toward boundary-free missions of love and understanding. Empaths also often identify with self-congratulatory posts of the "I can't help feeling your pain, but you shouldn't resent me for it, because that hurts my feelings and anyway this is who I am", sentiment.

Even the Emotionally Unavailable are recognized and accepted with posts declaring "I wish I could give one damn" and videos of dejected pugs, with rumpled bedsheets tucked up around their drooly muzzles, sleeping through yet another Monday. This last population is particularly interesting, as theoretically numb and "unavailable" humans can still identify with the very inertia that should render them unable to comprehend or respond at all!

And yes, the Emotionally Enlightened are included on social media too, albeit too often as an unattainable, elusive fantasy creatures, grasped tentatively for just a moment, taunting you with their perfection, as you watch them fade away from your earthbound, lesser selves.

I guess what confuses me is the groupthink Facebook mentality of accepting the Id Intelligent, the Empath and even the Emotionally Unavailable as necessary evils in our society. I declare that they are ALL unfinished states of Emotional Intelligence, and that these identities should be viewed as temporary waystations, in the journey towards Emotional Enlightenment.

I for one, don't want to spend the rest of my life in an emotionally inert state. Nor do I desire my massage therapist to be a sacrificial lamb, or the leader of my country to be obsessed with his own emotional agenda! I think we need to turn our current societal norms upside down. Never settle for emotional imbalance! Seek the balance of emotional enlightenment for all!

And with that said, I invite you to the next chapter of this book, where I will explore the possible reasons for your current position on the EI spectrum, and how you can begin to prepare yourself to reset and reposition yourself towards a path of growth and enlightenment.

The reasons we are positioned where we are on the EI Spectrum

How Did I End Up Here?

Now that you have a better idea of where you are positioned on the EI spectrum, it is time to figure out why you are at this point. Like anything else in life, every person has a unique life journey, but there are patterns and trends that can help us understand some of the more twisted bits of our path.

The Mind/Body Connection: What it is, Why it sometimes Disconnects, How to Reconnect it

Let's start with a physiological phenomenon called the mind/body connection. Basically, this is the intuitive connection between how the body reacts to or "feels" about an action, and what your mind thinks about the same action. If this system is connected properly, the body and the mind should work together so that you have the most current and accurate information about stimulus in your environment. The following are examples of the mind/body connection:

Stimulus 1: It is -10 degrees outside

Body: Arms and legs shake; teeth chatter. Body Feels Cold.

Mind Thinks: I am cold, I need to get warm.

Stimulus 2: Hot burner on stove

Body: Finger is burning. Body feels heat and pain.

Mind Thinks: I am hurt. I need medical attention.

Stimulus 3: Final exam that hasn't been studied for

Body: Stomach is churning. Body feels cramps and heartburn.

Mind Thinks: I am anxious. I should have studied!

Stimulus 4: Fiancé has broken off engagement

Body: Heart "aches"; body feels heavy, yet weak.

Mind Thinks: I am sad. My fiancé dumped me.

All these examples represent a mind/body connection that is running properly. There is an unbroken process between the stimuli, what the body feels and what the mind thinks.

So what does a mind/body disconnect look like?

Stimulus 1: It is 80 degrees in the bedroom

Body: Covered in perspiration, body feels hot.

Mind Thinks: Why am I having night sweats? Do I have cancer or am I going through menopause?

Stimulus 2: There is a crack in the pavement. You trip

Body: Falls and scrapes knee. Body feels nothing.

Mind Thinks: Huh? Ok, Ok I'm fine… (twenty minutes later) Why is there blood on my pants?

Stimulus 3: Someone in the subway car has a knife.

Body: Adrenaline flushes through body. Body is on alert.

Mind Thinks: I can't move. It's like I'm watching a movie…

Stimulus 4: Nothing

Body: Heart is racing. Vision is narrowing. Body feels dizzy

Mind: What is going on? I think I'm having a heart attack!

The examples above not only illustrate mind/body disconnects, but show that this disconnect can happen in a variety of ways. The bottom line: the mind and the body are not working together when the stimulus occurs, the body may not be feeling what it should, the mind may not be thinking what it should, and sometimes the mind and the body are reacting to a seemingly nonexistent stimulus, otherwise known as a panic attack.

When the mind/body connection is interrupted, re-routed or otherwise broken, we immediately become more vulnerable, less able to identify and control our own emotions, and much less or even incapable of processing the emotions of those around us. If this happens regularly, it's no wonder we go into defensive modes such as Id Intelligence, Emotional Empath or Emotionally Unavailable. Once we begin to identify with one or more of these EI Spectrum points, everything locks in and we are thrown into an increasingly vicious cycle of missed mind/body cues and inappropriate reactions to our own emotions; never mind the emotions of others.

So Why Does This Happen?

There are many theories about why the mind/body connection breaks down, and we find ourselves in a less than desirable position on the EI spectrum, but there is one factor in common: some form of lasting upset or disruption has occurred each and every time our EI balance is thrown off kilter. I am using extreme care when I choose the words "upset" or "disruption" to describe these events. It would be easier and more succinct to say "trauma", but I hesitate because trauma is a loaded and overused word to many people. Whatever the label, it is important to understand that changes in EI identity don't happen without a reason.

Some people believe that our EI identity is shaped and assigned to us in early childhood; the result of childhood "wounds". This theory suggests that these wounds start patterns and trends that follow us throughout our lives. If this resonates with you, there are many good books and material online about this.

Other theories believe that trauma can happen to anyone at any point in their lives. Whether through a one-time event, multiple incidents over a period of time, a lifetime of abuse or even multigenerational and/or cultural conditioning, there will always be an echo or ripple effect in that individual's emotional intelligence. Education and research are never a bad idea, when deconstructing how our past is playing out our present, and we are fortunate to live in an age of readily available and exhaustive material on trauma in its many forms and its repercussions.

I will wind up this chapter with three major types of life disruptions and how they may manifest in Emotional Intelligence spectrum positioning.

Situational Disruptions

Any disruption that is tied to a specific place, time or environment and results in EI imbalance can be grouped under the umbrella of Situational Disruptions. It is important to note that the origin of the situational disruption can be transferred to other, similar situations, i.e., if the individual who reacted to a situational disruption when they were 20 years of age, finds themselves **in what they construe** is a similar situation two decades later, the original disruption can transfer to the new but similar situation.

Examples of Situational Disruptions:

- Active duty in a warzone
- Bullied in Middle School
- Humiliated at a dance
- Forgot words to a song onstage
- Fled country as political refugee
- Systematically harassed at a job
- Eyewitness to a terror attack
- Almost drowned
- Choked on a sandwich
- Lived through a house fire
- Ridiculed in a presentation
- Dumped at a football game
- In a car accident at dawn

Important note about the examples listed above: The perceived random "seriousness" of these examples is purposeful. It is crucial when on the path of emotional enlightenment to understand that you don't get to judge what is an important enough event to affect you or others, and what is trivial or irrelevant. It simply doesn't matter. What does matter is that the event resonated with the individual and resulted in a shift in their EI balance.

Relational Disruptions

Any disruption that due to a relationship between 2 or more people and results in EI imbalance can be grouped under the umbrella of Relational

Disruptions. It is important to note that the origin of the original relational disruption can be transferred to other, similar relationships, i.e., if the individual who reacted to a relational disruption when they were 20 years of age, finds themselves **in what they construe** is a similar relationship two decades later, the original disruption can transfer to the new but similar relationship.

Examples of Relational Disruptions:

- In a Marriage broken up by cheating spouse
- Caring for someone you love in home hospice
- Assisting roommate through home detox
- Caring for someone you hate in home hospice
- Falling in love with someone with an addiction issue
- Being sexually harassed by a group of executives at work
- Being the child of a domestic abuser
- Covering for a coworker who is breaking company rules
- Discovering your daughter has stolen money from you
- Being made to choose which parent to live with
- Having an order of protection drawn against you from your grandchildren

- Raising a medically fragile child

Important note about the examples listed above: I think it becomes quite obvious that when the ingredients of a disruption include two or more people, it gets "personal" really fast. It doesn't matter if the disruption is caused by someone in need, someone in crisis, someone who intends malice, someone who is diseased or someone who is a victim, the results are consistently intense, life changing and unforgettable.

Transitional Disruptions:

Any disruption that due to a life transition and results in EI imbalance can be grouped under the umbrella of Transitional Disruptions. It is important to note that the origin of the original transitional disruption can be transferred to other, similar relationships, i.e., if the individual who reacted to a transitional disruption when they were 20 years of age, finds themselves **in what they construe** is a similar transition two decades later, the original disruption can transfer to the new but similar transition.

Examples of Transitional Disruptions:

- Retiring from a career
- Having a baby

- Empty Nest Syndrome, children have grown up and left home
- Growing up and leaving parents
- Starting a new career
- Being fired
- Dealing with teens
- Experiencing a midlife crisis
- Living through a loved one's midlife crisis
- Getting old
- Dealing with sudden physical limitations
- Living with a chronic illness
- Moving to a new town

Important note about the examples listed above: When it comes to transitional disruptions, it's a pretty safe bet that if you participate at all in this crazy process called life, you can't avoid at least a couple of these transitions. It's important to recognize when you are in the middle of one of these transition events, because the knowledge will help you conserve your energy for the long haul. Like all things, this too shall pass.

All three types of disruptions I have explored in this chapter can result in positional shifts in the EI Spectrum. If you refer back to the test you took at the beginning of this book, you may notice a shift in your answer choice throughout the test. What I didn't tell you is that the test was sectioned in four parts, focusing on work, friends, family and self. If there is a shift in test answers between these sections, it is most likely because of a situational, relational or transitional disruption. The good news is, with self-awareness, preparation, and armed with the proper tools, these same types of disruptions can also be transformed into opportunities for growth and Emotional Enlightenment, the apex of the EI spectrum, in all walks of your life.

Reconnect, Reset, Reposition!

You are now at the point in this book where you should know where on the EI spectrum you are currently positioned and have a pretty good idea of why and how you got there. Now we will explore the concepts of reconnecting your mind and body and resetting your positional potential; all in preparation for growth and EI spectrum repositioning!

Reconnect:

Before I tell you ways you can reconnect your mind/body connection, I should explain to you WHY this is such an important repair. The obvious reason is like any well calibrated system, if one or more cogs in the wheel aren't functioning, the whole system suffers. As I illustrated in the previous chapter, when the mind/body connection is fully functioning the results are elegantly simple: Action. Physical Reaction. Appropriate Thought Process. When the mind/body connection breaks down the results are random, chaotic and lack resolution: Action, perceived or actual. Variable and unreliable physical reaction. Thought process which may or may not be based in reality, appropriate place or time. In other words; Emotional Upheaval.

But there's an even more pressing reason to reconnect the mind and body. In order to take the first step on the path toward Emotional Enlightenment, you need to be present, or in the moment. And if your mind and body aren't working together, you can never count on being able to access PRESENCE. Without presence, there is no progression.

So how can you repair the mind/body connection? There are so many ways! These include Meditation, Mindfulness, Body Work, Energy Work, Guided Imagery, Grounding, Reflexology, Reiki, Chakra Point Work, Improvisation Classes, Yoga, and Thai Chi just to name a few. I urge you to do your research thoroughly before you choose a method and spend money. We are so fortunate to live in the era of the Internet, where information about the mind/body connection is plentiful and you can watch a video, or listen to a meditation or guided imagery experience for free to see if it resonates with you. These methods are highly individual and NONE of them will work without your personal buy-in.

And what does 'being in the moment" or Presence feel like? Again, personal experience is highly individual but generally when you are present or in the moment, you should have an overall sense of wellbeing. There should be a sense of Flow between your physical actions and your accompanying thoughts. You should feel grounded, literally like your feet are planted solidly on the ground you stand upon, and energy is flowing up out of your foundation and through the center of your body. You should feel connected to other people around you. Conversation should ebb and flow easily. Pauses are natural and comfortable.

Sometimes it's easier to comprehend what something SHOULDN'T feel like. Being present or in the moment isn't:

- Multi-Tasking
- Regretting the Past (Depression)
- Worrying about the Future (Anxiety)
- Self-editing
- Feeling Distracted

- Feeling like you are looking down at yourself from a distance
- Planning
- Predicting
- Projecting
- Feeling Awkward
- Experiencing physical distress, i.e., tunnel vision, lump in throat, difficulty breathing, etc.

Once you have achieved Presence through a repaired mind/body connection, you are ready to proceed to the next step of the process.

Reset:

When you make the decision to hit the reset button on your journey through the EI spectrum you need to be ready to reset your attitude, your previous knowledge and your expectations. If you are successful in the resetting process, you will receive one of the greatest gifts of all: the gift of POSSIBILITY. Possibility changes all the rules. Possibility allows you to entertain thoughts of improvement, enhancement and progression. Possibility opens the door to a sense of openness. If you can be open to change, to the chance that someone else's feelings might be as important or even more important than your own, to the option of letting someone else take the wheel for a minute, then my friend, before you know it you might just find yourself on the path to Emotional Enlightenment! Who knows? Anything is POSSIBLE!

PRESENCE+ POSSIBILITY = RESILIENCE

Reposition:

I think it's fair to ask, at this point, what's the big take way from all of this risky stuff like being in the moment, being present with your feelings, being open to possibility and abandoning previous assumptions. It may indeed feel, at this early stage like doing all of these things might make you feel weaker and more vulnerable, and, really, isn't that why you became emotionally imbalanced in the first place? I want to reassure you, that scary as all of this may sound, it will actually make you stronger. The simple reason is that if you have PRESENCE, then you open yourself to POSSIBILITY. Believing that future success is a possibility reveals the final gift behind the now unlocked door. That gift is RESILIENCEY.

Resiliency is the single most powerful weapon when fighting trauma. Resiliency gives you the strength to fight back. Resiliency gives you the ability to bounce back from bad experiences with a new vigor and energy. Resilience is your very essence, saying, NO. This is not how my story ends. I deserve a redo and I'm going to take every opportunity for growth and enlightenment that I can. I have a choice. I can choose to remain where I've landed, resigning myself to my present state of emotional imbalance. Or, I can choose to reconnect my mind and body and be in the moment, reset my attitude and expectations to possibility and reposition myself on the EI Spectrum, towards enlightenment, because I honor my resiliency.

I don't know about you, but I know what choice I'd make.

Let's refer one last time to trees. Think of an older tree. It's trunk is twisted, and scarred by storms, disease and predators, and there is a large hole where a branch must have been torn off at some point. There is no argument that this tree has been permanently altered from whatever caused this damage. Yet the tree continues to grow toward the sky, living for the day, preparing for the possibility of the future. That is resilience.

Before you progress to the second part of this book, which is all about implementing everything discussed in this first section in every aspect of your life, including your career, business and personal relationships, family dynamics and self-improvement, I want to add three caveats.

DENIAL, DISTRACTION AND DRUDGERY

The three "D"s. These 3 words represent impediments to your future emotional enlightenment. Avoid any state of mind willing to let these three words in. When you are Emotionally Unavailable, you have entered into a pact with Denial. Denial impedes you from ever making positive change because when you are in a state of denial, you don't have to face anything. This includes being in the moment, entertaining possibility and building resilience. When you are an Emotional Empath, you have agreed to a prescription of distraction. Distraction keeps you so busy with everyone else's needs, feelings and desires that it impedes you from ever accessing your own. When you are in a state of distraction, you don't have the time or energy to be present, believe in possibility and access the resilience to finally say NO. When you operate in Id Intelligence mode, you live in a constant, irritating state of drudgery. Drudgery impedes you from getting out of your defensive, "Me first" rut, because when your life is full of drudgery, you can't help but be insensitive and defensive. Why would you bother being in THAT moment, ever believe that anything was possible or exchange your coat of protective hubris for the shiny new armor of resiliency?

Part Two:

A Practical Implementation Guide

You have now come to the exciting part of my book where you learn how to put into practice everything you learned about in the first part. I have divided this part of the book into three chapters: Business and EI, Work/Personal Relationships and EI and Self-Improvement and EI. Each of these sections will include many step by step guides, showing you specific EI techniques to employ in various situations you may find yourself in. As you learn these techniques you will become more and more at ease with all of your emotional reactions and also realize how vitally important it is to be in controlled touch with your feelings in order to react to life's situational, relational and transitional challenges.

When I was growing up, and specifically, where I was growing up in New England, it was very in vogue to deny and hide your feelings! Feelings were considered an embarrassment and a sign of weakness. Boys didn't cry. Women were ridiculed for being "emotional". Everyone was told in direct and indirect ways to repress their feelings. Imagine an entire population spending all of their waking hours striving to be Emotionally Unavailable! But that was the culture.

It's a new millennium and we've come a long way, but the cultural mores of the past remain, as an undercurrent and a past form of conditioning that can crop up again and again when we are faced with a challenging situation, relationship or transition. That's why it is so important during these potentially stressful times to check in and make sure that none of these old cultural norms are chiding and rebuking us at the back of our minds. In turn, when dealing with others who seem to be at an emotional disconnect, we have to be mindful of the cultural voices that might be admonishing and mocking them!

Please read, think about, talk about and practice the techniques I have listed in the following pages. If you gradually incorporate them into your life, they will become part of you, a part that will help you to connect with yourself and others in ways you never dreamed possible.

Business EI

The very first step to incorporating Emotional Intelligence into your place of business is to do an initial EI spectrum inventory. This will be fun and very revealing! List all the people you supervise, work with and for, and assign them each an EI spectrum position. (EU/EE/ee/II). This will give you an immediate insight into what your business challenges will be, as well as give you so much more understanding of why your coworkers act the way they do. It may also start to change the way you "feel" about them and how you interact with them.

Next, make a list of all the current situational, relational and transitional disruptions you currently face at your job. Include the specific reports, co-workers and management that are involved in each of these disruptions. Now review these disruptions one by one, through the lens of the EI spectrum and with your new knowledge of the EI identities each of the people involved present. Are you surprised at how much clearer the real problems in these disruptions are? Can you envision specific interventions and resolutions for these disruptions that never would have occurred to you before your own emotional enlightenment?

For extra credit, try and identify disruptions that you are not involved in, observe the people who are involved and how their EI spectrum identities are affecting the situation. Imagine how you would intervene if you had a magic wand. This is great practice and could be preparing you for future management challenges!

Armed with this EI "map" of your workplace, it's time to explore and learn about specific work related scenarios and how you can master these challenges with emotional enlightenment!

EI and Leadership

If you are in a leadership position, you should first turn the EI lens on yourself and the people who directly report to you. You've already assigned EI identities to everyone involved and have also reviewed any current disruptions so you already have a pretty good idea how and why things are going. Now, as you move forward in an emotionally enlightened state, how can you be a better, fairer, more effective leader? I think, in any job you do, no matter your position in the hierarchy, in order to be in the moment, it is key to identify goals for every part of your day. In my other line of work as a licensed massage therapist, this is very easy. At the beginning of every session, after I've assessed the client's needs, as I ground myself, I mentally define a goal for the session, i.e., "I will release this client's left shoulder so he can work as a painter without pain". Mentally work out the different events of your workday; meetings, one on ones, presentations, etc., and give yourself a single goal for each one.

Next, once you have begun the interaction, ask everyone present what their goal is. Don't be judgmental about the answers. You are information gathering, not looking for the right answer. Think of the EI test you took at the beginning of this book. Individual goal responses may very well tell you where each and every one of your co-workers are on the EI spectrum in real time! If someone can't give you an answer, don't press it, but note to yourself that this person is currently emotionally unavailable and may need extra help or supervision. Notice how I said supervision, not discipline. Semantics are an important element in emotionally intelligent leadership. Thoughtful word choices can make the difference in any disruption or interaction. You don't need to lead by intimidation, domination or aggression. While it is an unfortunate reality that some people get promoted to leadership positions because their id intelligent behavior is perceived by others as forceful or "tough", their reigns are often tumultuous and characterized by direct reports and co-workers trying to topple them off their thrones. It is much more effective in the long run to be an enlightened leader, to say nothing of your job security!

As a leader your overarching goal should always be to model enlightened behavior, no matter how heated the disruption might be. This of course, can be very challenging but is a wonderful opportunity to improve your EI work in practice.

Even leaders have to report to someone above them in the business food chain. I am always amazed when someone who is a good leader turns out to be a bad report to their superior. Why does this happen? I think it's most likely a situational disruption that is at fault. Sometimes natural leaders have a weak spot when it comes to anyone criticizing them, real or assumed. Any directive, suggestion or comment can be misconstrued as criticism to someone who has a situational emotional imbalance. In that moment the leader, who is usually emotionally enlightened, shifts toward id intelligence because he "feels" that he is being criticized by his superior. If this same leader would take a step back, breathe, and reconnect he would soon realize that he has misconstrued the comment, that is actually, however awkwardly posed, an important goal of his superior.

If you are not currently in a leadership role at work, it is still very valuable to understand how and why leaders operate and this will, at the very least, improve your day-to-day work interactions with them. Whether it is part of your official title or not, we are all leaders of our emotional intelligence. When we are synced into where we are on the EI spectrum, we can more easily control our work interactions and disruptions.

EI and Workflow

The best way to approach workflow in the business place from an EI perspective is to equate it to the mind/body connection. The minute I hear the word "flow" in any context my go to place is the mind/body connection. There are articles, books and documentaries about flow. Basically flow represents a state of being where the mind/body connection is so fluid and transparent that every action of one's day is filled with ease, unconscious yet logical progression and a sense of well-being. As such, who wouldn't make that the primary goal of business workflow?

In the mind/body connection, there is an initial stimulus, a physical reaction and a coordinating thought process. In business workflow, there is an initial work request, an individual and/or team response, and the finished product. Let's deconstruct this process and see where there could be a disconnect. In the business model of today, it is quite possible that workflow is created and generated using a computer program. This streamlines the process, cuts down on manpower hours and formulates the process so that there is consistency, benchmarks and an automated, date-driven mode of operation. However, as we all know, a computer is only as smart as its data input. Even with advances in technology, this process depends on individuals and/or teams to do the work necessary for a final product. So before anything else, you will need to identify the EI spectrum positions of everyone involved in the workflow. Then you need to cross reference the identity with the job they are responsible to accomplish. Finally you need to look at past performance and pinpoint disruptions, as well as where and when in the workflow process they occurred. When you have done these three steps, you should have quite an accurate picture of how well the workflow process is running, as well as weak spots and disconnects. This will give you an opportunity to address the disruptions, supervise and guide those individuals whose EI spectrum identities are not meshing well with their job responsibilities and even reassign and reposition both people and steps in the process to make it run smoother. And the irony of this whole analysis is that by using Emotional Intelligence, you end up with solutions that are objective and easy to implement without getting angry or blaming anyone. It's a systemic solution to a systemic process!

EI and Networking

I have a confession to make. I don't like to network and for many years I couldn't figure out why. I blamed it on other people's attitudes, trying to pretend a business event was a social event, and the fact that I'm in introvert. If all else failed, and I had to go, I would drag a friend, hit the bar and the apps table and retreat to a dark corner with them where we would remain until the end of the event, in complete oppositional denial!

Now that I have embraced emotional enlightenment, I can look at this scenario though the EI lens:

I have a confession to make. I don't like to network and this is why. When I feel stressed, and this type of event makes me feel stressed, my emotional intelligence spectrum position veers toward being an emotional empath. Networking reminds me of when I was growing up and had difficulties mixing with more than one friend at a time or having to mix new friends with old friends. I was so concerned with them all getting along, that I couldn't relax and be in the moment. The more I worried the less connected I was to the people I was supposed to be interacting with until I completely repositioned my EI identity to Emotionally Unavailable. If I am forced to go to a networking event, my inclination is to drag one friend with me, fill up on drinks and apps and sit in a corner, effectively physically, mentally and spiritually declaring my unavailability to network.

One Scenario interpreted through two different lenses. The first scenario is a story about the fact I hate networking, I give excuses, I come up with an escape plan, but at the end of the day I don't know WHY I hate networking. The second scenario is also a story about the fact I hate networking. I give an emotionally intelligent explanation of why this is and I refer it back to a situational/relational experience from my youth. I even explain through the EI lens, why I have devised an escape plan.

If I choose to improve, the second scenario gives me a wealth of information to work with, in my desire to network better. It gives me the understanding that it's not the event that is problematic, but how I relate to it. It points out that if try to stay in the moment, remember that my goal is to meet people and talk about work relationships with them I might actually enjoy the event. It also guides me to wonder how other people feel about networking events. Finally it objectively shows me that if I stop overthinking all the reasons I don't like to interrelate with groups of people and follow the process naturally set in place, by the very nature of the event, I should be able to actually succeed at networking!

The key elements of networking:

- When networking try to be in the moment.
- Go with the goal of meeting new people and talking about work relationships.
- Understand that everyone there is also trying to network, despite the EI identities they might be presenting.
- Don't go to a networking event with Id Intelligence. You won't learn anything.
- Don't go to a networking event as an Emotional Empath. You won't remember anything.
- Don't go to a networking event if you are Emotionally Unavailable. You won't be there anyway.

EI and Conflict Resolution

Here's a funny thing about conflict in the work environment. Yes it can be devastating, ruining your day, your sleep that night and bleeding over into every facet of your life. But it shouldn't because it's a work conflict. It's not personal. It doesn't involve your family or loved ones. It's work. Therefore, when work conflict plays out in a correct, controlled manner it should actually feel relatively safe.

The most important fact you should know before participating in a work conflict is how you feel. When you check in with yourself to find out how you feel, you have to be brutally honest with yourself. You also have to figure out WHY you feel as you do. It's not enough to check in, find out you're furious and storm into the meeting. In fact, that's exactly what you shouldn't do. Once you determine exactly how you feel and also why you feel that way, you then need to decide if this emotion is appropriate to the control of its intensity. This is the initial assessment when preparing to participate in any form of conflict. In the instance of work place conflict, you need to remember that you are participating in conflict in a professional environment and your actions may result in both positive and negative repercussions that could directly affect your future employability. The good news is that it's still about work – it should never be personal.

Once you are actively engaged in work place conflict, it is essential that you keep checking in with yourself for several reasons. First, you need to keep checking that you are actively present. Not planning, not rationalizing, and not plotting. In the moment. Can you see and feel how the other participants are reacting? If you can, then you are present. If you can't or don't care, you are not. Next you need to keep taking your emotional temperature and deciding if you can handle the heat. If you can't you need to step away. Stepping away means just that. Take a step back. Breathe. Collect yourself. Actively listen for a while. None of this needs to be dramatic. You don't need to run out of the room. You just need to shift gears. An interesting byproduct of stepping away is that it may very well shift the dynamic of the conflict. Remember the goal of workplace conflict is always professional resolution.

Let's run though the steps of this process:

- Initial check in: Are you present? How do you feel? Why do you feel the way you do? Is your feeling appropriate to the conflict? Can you control this emotion during conflict?
- Check in while participating in conflict: Are you still present? How do you feel now? Can you see and feel how other participants are doing? Can you control the intensity of your emotions during this conflict? If yes, continue. If No
- Step away: Take a step back, sit, actively listen, shift focus
- Has goal been accomplished? Is there a professional resolution?

EI and Career Path

The short and sweet version of this segment is that if you've read and followed all the other EI Business topics presented here you should be firmly positioned on the career path of success.

While that may be true, let's take a moment or two to flesh this out.

The words 'career path' make me think of the EI spectrum path. For both, I think it's so important that you know where you starting point is and have an end goal in sight at all times. The end goal may shift, change, veer off the original path or branch out on a new path, but as long as growth is always happening and balance is maintained, the sky is the limit.

We've explored leadership and EI. I think the takeaway is that no matter where you are on your career path, it's never too early to start thinking like a leader, nor is there ever a point where you can stop your quest for leadership enlightenment. Also, you have to be cognizant of the organization as a whole, a living, breathing organism made up of the people it employs and the gifts they bring. "Cog in the wheel" mentality is what causes disconnects on a career path. It signifies an inability to relate to others. It signifies a lack of natural curiosity, necessary for growth of any kind. It results in being Emotionally Unavailable.

We've made a connection between work flow and the mind/body connection. Anyone who is seriously on a career path and has an organic understanding of work flow process is sure to be noticed and promoted. We've discussed networking; why it's necessary; how it need not be unpleasant and how to approach it from an EI perspective. Any human resources professional worth their salt will tell you that networking gets people more employment, job growth and business opportunities because it is a hands-on, face-to-face intrapersonal experience, Finally, we've gone step by step through the process of workplace conflict, deconstructing what is and isn't appropriate, establishing boundaries and learning how to monitor our emotional temperature. All of these techniques will serve you well as you traverse a career path. Perhaps, more importantly they lay the foundation for, and transference of EI skills that will help your business and personal relationships flourish.

Work/Personal Relationships and EI

In the last chapter we dealt with situational and relational disturbances that can take place in business environments. In this chapter we will deal more with relational and transitional disturbances that can occur in relationships of all kinds, throughout the many stages of our lives.

Before we begin, you will need to add to a list you started in the last chapter. Take a look at your initial EI workplace inventory and pull out the EI spectrum position list of everyone you work with.

You will need these as you work on Business Relationships. Now make a list of all of your friends and family, assigning them each an EI spectrum position. You will need these as you work on Personal Relationships. We are now ready to begin this chapter.

Using EI to Influence Others

Why would you ever want to influence other people? At the outset, I wouldn't be surprised if you asked me this question. Isn't it wrong to talk people into things? Isn't it a form of manipulation or very self-serving? The short answer: it all depends.

If you are reading this book because you want the secret to unlocking the power to get people to give you all their money, or rob a bank or smuggle drugs over the border for you, then you have come to the wrong place. Basically, your motivation is unethical and comes from a negative place and using the techniques I have discussed in this book for your ill-gotten gain, would, in an ideal world, result in a huge amount of bad karma. If, however, you would like some pointers on how to sell your company's latest product, or get your church to agree to spend money on the pipe organ, or convince the PTA to fundraise for a new playground, or talk your wife and 3 teenagers into taking that vacation of a lifetime, you've come to the right place!

The word "influence" has gotten a bad rap over the years, starting with the 60s self-help gurus touting how to win friends and influence people, and continuing with shady politicians, paid off to influence voting decisions and inflate the price of pork bellies. Historically however, the word influence conjures up wise men of letters who were of great influence and weighed in on important issues. Beloved leaders who were responsible for influencing decisions that ended world wars, sent men to the moon and ended slavery. When I use the word "influence" in this book, I mean THAT kind of influence.

In order to influence people in business or in your personal life, you need their buy-in. This means, you need to ensure that they strongly agree with the proposition you are attempting to make. This is where the EI spectrum comes into play. Pick up those lists of business associates and friends and family that identify each of their EI spectrum positions. In order to influence someone, you need to know where they are coming from. What better way to start than through the lens of the Emotional Intelligence spectrum. If you know where people appear to be positioned on the spectrum you also get all sorts of insight, into what motivates them, how prepared they are to be influenced, and how much work it's going to take to get to know what they are passionate about. If they are emotionally enlightened, they are going to be very open to new things. If they are Emotional Empaths they are going to be very concerned about the need and desires of others, but will be thrilled if asked and given the time to decide about what they'd like. If they are Id Intelligent they are going to demand to know, "What's in it for ME", and if they are Emotionally Unavailable you are going to have to put in some work, observing what DOES put a sparkle in their eyes. (This last technique will be as necessary for surly unavailable teens, nonverbal toddlers and the elderly who suffer from dementia, as it is for the uninspired apathetic worker.) Basically, you need to know your audience and the EI spectrum is as good as any place to start.

Once you know your audience, you need to ensure their buy in through appealing to who they are, what they feel passionately about and how your proposition will give them gratification. Everyone has something they care about whether it is as altruistic as feeding hungry orphans or as self-serving as getting the neighbors next door in trouble for improper recycling. It's your job to identify where they are on the EI spectrum and to find out what makes them tick.

Using EI to be a Better Communicator

If you've mastered how to use EI to influence others, you're already well on your way to becoming a better communicator. You've learned how to get to know your audience, where they are on the EI spectrum and what motivates them in life.

In order to be a better EI communicator you also need to always have a goal, as well as to recognize the goals of the people you want to communicate with and finally, how to bridge, scaffold and/or support everyone's goals so you are addressing motivated listeners. The fastest way to turn an apathetic audience into motivated listeners is to talk to their issues. This is where doing your homework on past collective and specific disturbances will always pay off.

If you are trying to talk to parents about school safety, you have to research past situational, relational and transitional disturbances that have occurred in their district and it will be even more powerful if you can reference specific disturbances to specific audience members. Your goal is to prove to these people that you know their issues. Their goal is to make sure you hear about the disturbances that are important to them. You, as the successful EI communicator need to ultimately bridge all of your goals together as you communicate your solutions to the school safety problem.

When it comes to communicating better with family, it's initially easier, because you are very well versed in their individual EI spectrum positions, collective and specific disturbances, but ultimately it is harder, because the stakes are higher. This is your family, your tribe. Your goal needs to always include reconciliation because these are the most important people in your life.

Work Relationships and EI

When it comes to work relationships, the shade of grey always comes in to play. When I wrote earlier about using emotional intelligence in business, I focused on the hierarchy, processes and routines, conflict and career paths of the work environment. I also tried to point out that when it comes to emotions in the work place, it's always a good idea to check in frequently and make sure the emotions you are experiencing are appropriate to a professional work environment and that you are confident that you can control the intensity of the emotion while participating in work events. I also said to always remember that it's work and it's not personal. I only wish it was as easy to live by these words as it is to write them.

If work were just a series of processes and routines, we could all clock in and out on automatic pilot and that would be that. But we are not machines. We are human beings. And when you put more than one human being together in a controlled environment you always get relational disturbances. Always.

So we bring in the concept of boundaries. Good Boundaries are the peacemakers of the business environment. But you have to recognize them, respect them and refrain from jumping over, crawling under or skulking around them at all times. A boundary is a mental fence that delineates the borders of acceptable behavior. Unfortunately, it is an unfortunate facet of human nature that many people spend countless hours of their lives trying to ignore, shift or break down perfectly good work boundaries. I have a theory about this behavior. I think that when people aren't emotionally intelligent, they sublimate their desire to feel things by destroying boundaries in an attempt, negative though it might be, to feel ANYTHING AT ALL. An Emotionally Unavailable employee will literally sleepwalk through boundaries all the day long, showing up late for meetings, falling asleep at their desks, losing their place in a presentation. They are huge passive aggressive boundary breakers. An Emotional Empath will constantly push and pull boundaries out of shape like a wet sweater, trying to meet the needs and desires of everyone around her, making emotional exceptions for others because she feels their pain. Then when the person she has been altering boundaries for gets in trouble and comes back at the empath, she will be devastated and confused, tearfully saying, "I was only trying to help". The Id Intelligent employee will ricochet off boundaries like a punch drunk boxer in a ring. Boundaries infuriate the id intelligent, who misconstrue them as prisons or walls meant to keep them away from what they desire.

The Emotionally Enlightened employee has a far different relationship with boundaries. He sees them as protective borders within which he is free to be creative, explore, learn and grow. What a difference enlightenment makes!

Wherever you are on path to emotional enlightenment, please take my advice: when it comes to work relationships, respect and adhere to the boundaries. They are your real business friends. If you respect work boundaries, you can enjoy many different work relationships, even those who become friends you see outside of work, as long as when you are both in work you mind the boundaries. It's that what happens in Vegas, stays in Vegas maxim. The friendship can exist fluidly in multiple environments but the participants in the friendship must adhere to the specific environment's rules. There is nothing worse than covering for a friend at work when you know they are wrong. And there is nothing less respectful than asking someone to cover for you at work, when you know you are wrong.

Friendships and EI

We've touched upon friendships in business, including those we become closer to and see outside of work. Now let's get to the heart of the matter and discover how the EI spectrum can help us make and keep friends.

Think of all the friends you've had throughout your life, even the ones you are no longer friends with. Write them all down on a list and assign them each an EI spectrum position. Now go back through the list and if you've had disturbances with any of them, note them, including whether it was situational, relational or transitional. If you are no longer friends, take a moment to ground, be in the moment and write down the reason why without overthinking it.

When you have reviewed this list do you see any patterns in the type of person you have chosen to be friends with. Are there friends who don't fit the pattern? Look at the types of disturbances you've had with your friends. Again, do patterns emerge? Finally look at the reasons why you are no longer friends with some of these people. Patterns?

I ask you to do this to get a clear picture of who attracts you as a friend, what you have conflict about with friends, and what would make you stop being friends with someone. I think these are all good things to know about yourself as you continue to go through life making friends. Yes, you should make friends throughout your life! I hear over and over again how you'll never meet the kind of friends you make when you are young…While this may be true, why does that stop you from making new, different friends; friends who may be more appropriate to the stage of life you are going through now?

Here's a touching and revealing story a client of mine once told me. Her dearest friend had died three years ago, sending her into a tailspin of grief that she had never experienced before in her life, including when her father and my mother, who she loved dearly, died. When she thought it through, she realized that she was really in mourning for her youth. As long as her best friend and she were both alive, time stood still for them. When he passed, not only did she have to come to grips with the loss of him; she had to also come to grips with saying goodbye to her early adulthood. At the grand old age of 53, she had to face reality and admit she was middle aged. After a suitable period of Emotional Unavailability, she emerged out the other side, with the realization that growth and enlightenment have no age limits. She began to open herself up to the possibility of making new friends, of all ages, to be the road companions on her personal EI path. Her ever increasing and diverse group of friends are a much more accurate reflection of who she is now and who she aspires to be. Her old friends make her feel cherished. Her new friends make her feel resilient.

Romantic Relationships and EI

When looking for a romantic partner, I've learned that a good test is to think of all my friends, and imagine the current man of my dreams interacting with all of them. Would knowing him enhance their lives? Would they be friends with him? If you had told me to do this when I started dating, I would have snapped, "Why would I? They're not marrying him!" Yet, now, sadder but wiser, I think its serious food for thought. I began to notice that my choice of romantic partners never became great friends with any of my friends. Eventually, this raised a red flag for me: Why was I dating men who I probably wouldn't be friends with? When looking for a romantic relationship, use your EI friendship template as a base line. If they could be friends with at least some of your friends and you are attracted to them, that's a fighting start.

Be in the moment. Have goals in mind when you are looking. Check in with yourself throughout the dating process. When you are with him do you generally have a sense of wellbeing? Do you feel like you've been to this rodeo before? Are there ways that he makes you feel or things that he does that remind you of a former love that ended badly?

I refuse to believe that we are destined to be attracted to one type of person and that we date them over and over like a mechanized doll wound up by Fate and his pal Karma! I do know that this happens to lots of people and have come to realize that it is a hallmark of ignoring or being unaware of an imbalance in their Emotional Intelligence.

I end this section with a few Dating Dos and Don'ts:

- Do date people who enhance the life you are already living.
- Don't date your reflection. Dating a looking glass partner will only send you down the rabbit hole.
- Do date people who are Emotionally Available.
- Don't date people who you think can fix you.
- Do date people who you like just as they are.
- Don't date people because you want to fix them.

Family Relationships and EI

When it comes to families, I think it's safe to say, there is no "right" or "wrong" way. Families are fascinating. Coming as I do from a very repressed New England family, full of ruggedly independent yet surprisingly creative types who loved each other in the strictest sense, but were honestly not that great at being a family, I've made it a ongoing pastime of mine to study families and figure out what makes the good ones work. I've known great families who lived like a pack of dogs, with an alpha male and a lively, happy pack that fell into line and flourished. I've known families who were very tribal, all over each other's lives with everything in common, and a common need to be with each other all the time. I've known crazy families, each member more eccentric than the other, all doing their own thing, yet making a greater whole in some random chaotic way. What did they all have in common? There was a baseline of mutual respect that was extended from the elders to the infants. There was a recognition that whatever the disturbance, be it situational, relational or transitional, their collective need for one another took precedence every time. And they were genuine. No one was playing a part. They were all present for each other in good times and bad.

The cool thing about all of the advice and tips, dos and don'ts, anecdotes and reminders in the sections above is they all work together, in an EI continuum. You can mix and match them, put them in any order, and you'll still come up with some great ways to bring EI into all of your relationships.

Self-Improvement EI

We've come to the last, but it no way the least important section of the implementation guide. Like so many things in life, it all comes down to you; and this is especially true through the EI spectrum lens, where if you only learn one thing, let it be that you will only be as good as the good you do for yourself.

It is an easily proven fact that if you are great at knowing how other people feel, what they want, and what they need, to the detriment of your own feelings, desires and needs, you will eventually burn out, exhausted from the anxiety of eternally projecting and resentful of those you've tried to fix. Hopefully this will be a wakeup call to reset your EI compass and reposition yourself toward emotional enlightenment. But as I've just as easily land you in the opposite direction of Id Intelligence or even becoming Emotionally Unavailable.

I end this implementation guide with a few techniques designed for self-improvement. Enjoy these EI gifts!

Using EI to be More Social

Back in the "EI for Networking" section I mentioned my dislike of networking and at one point blamed my being an introvert on my negative feelings. To tell you the truth, my aversion to networking has extended at times in my life to any sort of social gathering. In retrospect and through the lens of emotional enlightenment, I am now sure that my social anxiety was a byproduct of being an Emotional Empath, and that at its worst, reflected my downshifting into being Emotionally Unavailable, which served me quite well in the moment, but gave me nightmares later when I replayed the event in my head and couldn't remember one interaction!

Id Intelligence doesn't fare much better in the social arena. There is tremendous pressure for the ID intelligent to be "on" during social events, because his agenda needs to be endlessly communicated. This takes a great deal of energy, exhausting him at the best of times and fueling him with frustration and resentment when, despite his desperate efforts, he feels he wasn't heard.

Being social should never be anxiety ridden or energy depleting, but like anything else you want to be good at in life, you need to be prepared. And through the EI spectrum lens, this requires your presence, your openness to possibility and resilience.

Preparation steps to be more social:

- Make sure you are grounded and in the moment.
- Upon entering a social event, scan the room and take the EI temperature.
- Check in with your own feelings and see how they sync with the environment, Adjust as needed.
- Give yourself a simple goal and make a game out of meeting it. If you need material for small talk, you can even talk about it!

Using EI to be More Successful

If you read the section of this book focusing on Business EI, you probably picked up some great tips on how to be successful in the workplace. But life is more than work, and success should always be a presence in your life. Revisiting the mind/body connection and the state of wellbeing brought on by presence are valuable resources when in search of success throughout your day. It's hard to feel successful when you are worried about getting your needs met. It's hard to feel successful when you are fighting off an anxicty attack about something that happened two weeks ago. It's hard to feel successful when you don't even have the energy to sit up straight in your work chair. Now shift into Enlightenment mode and feel positivity fill you as you walk into a room, prepared with a goal, living in the moment, open to the possibility of success and armed with resilience, just in case it's not right around the corner. It all comes down to balance, and hitting that sweet spot on the EI spectrum.

Using EI to Gain Self-Control

Do you feel as though you have better self-control in some parts of your life than others? Are you known as laid back at work, but mean mom at home? Is it the opposite way around? If this is the case, you may be interested to know that it is quite common for people with self-control issues to also be compartmentalized, meaning that they live the different parts of their life in separate little boxes. Work box; home box; social box; etc. The obvious problem with this, coming from an EI perspective, is that you end up spending so much time and energy maintaining all these separate "residences" that you become depleted, and eventually assign one of the boxes to be the place you allow yourself to blow up. Read that explanation again and tell me about the part that sounds like a good idea!

In the EI for Conflict Resolution section, one of the specific steps to maintain control of your emotions during work conflict was to periodically check with your feelings as you participated, checking the appropriateness of the emotion as well as the intensity. If you believed you were still in control you could proceed. If not, you were to self-direct yourself to STEP AWAY. This last directive should be the mantra of anyone with self-control issues. STEP AWAY. SIT DOWN. BREATHE. SHIFT THE FOCUS. Let me add a few more tips here: modulate the tone and volume of your voice. Even better? Stop talking (yelling?) and just listen. Look around you. Look at how the people around you are reacting to your loss of self-control. What do they look like? What are they feeling? What are they saying? If you can't answer these questions because you are still flooded with emotion, leave the room. Remove yourself to a safe space until you have come back to your baseline.

I say all this with love and seriousness. If you would try to control yourself at work, what excuse would ever be good enough to explain NOT working to control yourself around friends, your parents, your partner or your children?

Using EI to be Fulfilled

Fulfillment. That ever elusive mecca of emotion! You know it's out there. You've had glimpses of it as you become emotionally enlightened. But how do you get it stay around and hang out with you?

I believe it comes down to finding your bliss. Doing that one thing that makes you feel like a kid again. That one thing you could do all day, every day. For me it's doing massage. When I'm in the zone, there is no sense of time, my energy flows, my body has a mind of its own and my mind is completely at peace. My world narrows to the space between my fingers and I finally understand the term "flow". What's your bliss? No need to be devastated if you don't have a ready answer. I didn't find mine until I was 50, but the good news is, once you find it, you can access it again and again.

So if you've found your bliss, then practice it every day you are able to. If not, prepare to find your bliss. Maintain your presence, open yourself to possibility and arm yourself with resilience. Your bliss is out there waiting for you. And where there's bliss, there's fulfillment.

Review and Summary

Interrelating your worlds into a cohesive whole

When I began this book, it became more and more clear to me how appropriate it was to depict the EI spectrum as circular rather than linear. A line signifies a beginning, a middle and an end; or when it is representing a spectrum one extreme, a middle state and another extreme. Emotional Intelligence follows neither of these descriptions. It is a fluid state, shifting back and forth, as we aspire to its balance of enlightenment. The visual image of how interwoven the trio of Id Intelligence, Emotional Enlightenment and Emotional Empath are serve as a cautionary reminder of how close an ideal state can be to an undesirable one. What a humbling concept that is!

You've learned about the mind/body connection and how important Presence is to Emotional Enlightenment. You've learned to be open to Possibility, and you've learned that our past experiences, rather than bringing us down, can with Presence and Possibility give us Resilience.

You've also been cautioned against the impediments of Denial, Distraction and Drudgery.

You can now identify not only your current EI position, but also the EI position of anyone else you interact with.

You understand the impact of disturbances on Emotional Intelligence, and can differentiate between situational, relational and transitional disturbances.

Now I urge you to take what you've learned in each of the specific areas or "worlds" that we covered in Business, Relationships and Self and work every day to interrelate these areas of your life into a cohesive whole.

An integral element of Emotional Enlightenment is Authenticity. In order to be your most Authentic self, you must be the same person no matter where you are, who you are with and what challenges you are facing. This is a lifetime challenge; an endless work in progress, but it is a worthy goal. Use environmental boundaries, such as those in the work place to keep your interactions appropriate. That way you don't have to change who you are to fit the place. Stay open when interacting with people who intimidate you or who you don't like, or who you wish you were more like. Instead of reacting to them in a negative or false manner or shutting down completely, listen to their story. You may find out something about them that will change your whole perception of who they are!

I have added a bonus chapter to this book, to help you with your lifelong journey towards Emotional

Enlightenment. It is a 30 day EI immersion program and it is designed to be used over and over again as a reference, refresher and EI touchstone. Good luck!

Bonus Chapter 30 Day EI Immersion Program

This program isn't meant to be progressive or finite. I think by now you know you can't be emotionally enlightened in a month's time! My hope is that it will be inspirational. The first time you use it you can go in order if you wish, but it was created more as a lifetime reference. Experience EI every day of your life and your journey will be a fulfilling adventure!

Day One: Go online and read about the mind/body connection. See if you can find an article or video or image that resonates with you.

Day Two: Check in with yourself every hour that you are awake today. Ask yourself what you are feeling and why.

Day Three: Try and keep a simple tally of every time you start to worry about something during the day. Later review it and ask WHY?

Day Four: Sit in a quiet room for 20 minutes. Using your senses, jot down everything you experienced.

Day Five: Research some form of mindfulness, meditation or relaxation technique that resonates with you. Don't spend any money until you have thoroughly read about it, and ideally, sampled it for free.

Day Six: Keep a list of disruptions you were involved in or observed today. Decide whether they were situational, relational or transitional.

Day Seven: Listen to a guided imagery session online.

Day Eight: Write down all the distractions that are currently in your life. See if there are any you can eliminate, either for a set period, or permanently.

Day Nine: Go on Facebook and see how many posts/pictures you can find that describe the four major EI positions on the EI spectrum. How do they make you feel?

Day 10: Go through magazines and cut out images that make you feel emotionally enlightened. Make an EE collage!

Day 11: Sit alone in a café or coffee bar and observe body language and nonverbal communication. Try not to listen to conversations, but see if you can figure out what people are talking about.

Day 12: Look around your office space and see if you can identify at least one of every EI spectrum position in your co-workers.

Day 13: Jot down what your career path goals are for the next year, using an EI lens.

Day 14: Instead of a Family Tree, make a family EI spectrum, plotting family members along the path. Notice patterns and trends.

Day 15: Listen to an online meditation session. Find a voice you like!

Day 16: Sit for 20 minutes and listen to music. Jot down how it makes you feel and why.

Day 17: Keep an emotions journal today. See now many emotions you experience in one day and how they affect you.

Day 18: Take a walk in nature and note what elements give you a sense of wellbeing.

Day 19: Ask a friend to try this with you: One of you will talk to the other for 5 minutes without interruption. Reflect back what you heard, check for accuracy. Switch.

Day 20: Write down the 5 most common reasons for a disruption in your family. Why?

Day 21: Think of a physical activity that you've done that puts you in the mindfulness zone; activities like swimming, running, rowing or yoga. Plan time to do this activity regularly, to clear your mind and bring you "into the moment".

Day 22: Think of three things that make you really angry. Why do they make you angry?

Day 23: If you can, spend 20 minutes with a nonverbal toddler today. If you can't, watch videos of them online. Can you figure out what they feel, want and/or need?

Day 24: Check your local entertainment section and find an improvisation show to go to in the future. Observe how it looks when people are in the moment and being funny! Alternative: watch improvisation videos on Youtube. Or take a class!

Day 25: Try a therapeutic breathing session online.

Day 26: Look at dating sites through an EI lens...

Day 27: Write down the 5 most common reasons for disruptions at work. Patterns?

Day 28. Look around your living space. How does it make you feel? Are there elements you could change for the better?

Day 29: Who is the most authentic person you know? Why?

Day 30: Write down 10 things that currently threaten your EI balance. Want can you change?

FREE DOWNLOAD

INSIGHTFUL GROWTH STRATEGIES FOR YOUR PERSONAL AND PROFESSIONAL SUCCESS!

Sign up here to get a free copy of Growth Games workbook and more:

www.frenchnumber.net/growth

You may also like...

EMOTIONAL INTELLIGENCE SPECTRUM

EXPLORE YOUR EMOTIONS AND IMPROVE YOUR INTRAPERSONAL INTELLIGENCE

BY JOSHUA MOORE AND HELEN GLASGOW

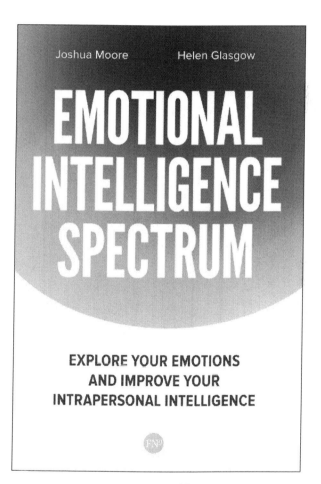

Emotional Intelligence Spectrum is the one book you need to buy if you've been curious about Emotional Intelligence, how it affects you personally, how to interpret EI in others and how to utilize Emotional Quotient in every aspect of your life.

Once you understand how EQ works, by taking a simple test, which is included in this guide, you will learn to harness the power of Emotional Intelligence and use it to further your career as you learn how to connect with people better.

You may also like...

I AM AN EMPATH

ENERGY HEALING GUIDE FOR EMPATHIC AND HIGHLY SENSITIVE PEOPLE

BY JOSHUA MOORE

I Am an Empath is an empathy guide on managing emotional anxiety, coping with being over emotional and using intuition to benefit from this sensitivity in your everyday life – the problems highly sensitive people normally face.

Through recongnizing how to control emotions you have the potential to make the most of being in tune with your emotions and understanding the feelings of people around you.

Begin your journey to a fulfilling life of awareness and support today!

You may also like...

MAKE ROOM FOR MINIMALISM

A PRACTICAL GUIDE TO SIMPLE AND SUSTAINABLE LIVING

BY JOSHUA MOORE

Make Room for Minimalism is a clear cut yet powerful, step-by-step introduction to minimalism, a sustainable lifestyle that will enable you to finally clear away all the physical, mental and spiritual clutter that fills many of our current stress filled lives. Minimalism will help you redefine what is truly meaningful in your life.

Eager to experience the world of minimalism?

Add a single copy of **Make Room for Minimalism** to your library now, and start counting the books you will no longer need!

FN℠

Presented by French Number Publishing

French Number Publishing is an independent publishing house headquartered in Paris, France with offices in North America, Europe, and Asia.

FN℠ is committed to connect the most promising writers to readers from all around the world. Together we aim to explore the most challenging issues on a large variety of topics that are of interest to the modern society.

FN℠

All rights Reserved. No part of this publication or the information in it may be quoted from or reproduced in any form by means such as printing, scanning, photocopying or otherwise without prior written permission of the copyright holder.

Disclaimer and Terms of Use: Effort has been made to ensure that the information in this book is accurate and complete, however, the author and the publisher do not warrant the accuracy of the information, text and graphics contained within the book due to the rapidly changing nature of science, research, known and unknown facts and internet. The Author and the publisher do not hold any responsibility for errors, omissions or contrary interpretation of the subject matter herein. This book is presented solely for motivational and informational purposes only.

Made in the USA
Lexington, KY
13 October 2017